A Classic Collection of Earl[y]

BLUES

for the Ukulele

Compiled by
Dick Sheridan

To access audio, visit:
www.HalLeonard.com/MyLibrary

Enter Code
2377-0603-3957-1686

Design & Typography by Roy "Rick" Dains
FalconMarketingMedia@gmail.com

ISBN 978-1-57424-341-3

Contents

The Author Reflects

For me, the introduction to the blues came with the 1949 Delmore Brothers recording of Blues, Stay Away from Me. Together with a high school friend, we'd play the song with our acoustic folk guitars, one laboring over the only three chords we knew, the other picking the melody on the single high E string. We certainly weren't ready for Prime Time, but it was a beginning.

Fast forward to college days when a campus jazz band was organized and I was recruited to play banjo. Problem was that I didn't know how to play the banjo. But I did play the ukulele, and that was good enough. A banjo mandolin was found, strings reduced from 8 to 4, and the instrument tuned to a baritone uke. It didn't take long before we discovered the blues songs that came from the treasury of early New Orleans jazz. Simple basic songs at first, like Canal Street Blues and Tin Roof Blues. Add to the mix a little "make up" blues, Frankie and Johnny, some Boogie Woogie, and for us what was old was new again.

Following graduation and military service, the blues lay dormant until I was introduced to a local group of amateur musicians eager to form a band and in need of a banjo player. Dixieland jazz was very popular at the time and a six-piece outfit was put together to fit the mold. Initially our tune list was limited but in time it gradually increased, no small part of which was the blues, many of them included in this collection. The band is still intact and active after over half a century with a wide variety of blues still forming an essential part of its repertoire.

Because of space and other restrictions some excellent blues couldn't be included in this collection but the reader is encouraged to seek them out. There's the Apex Blues by clarinetist Jimmie Noone; Wolverine Blues with Bix Beiderbecke; Jelly Roll Morton's Buddy Bolden's Blues; the Limehouse Blues with renditions by Django Reinhardt, Les Paul and Chet Atkins; Pete Seeger singing the Winnsboro Cotton Mill Blues; the Livery Stable Blues by the Original Dixieland Jazz Band; Louis Armstrong's celebrated introduction to West End Blues along with his contribution to Dippermouth Blues in King Oliver's Creole Jazz Band, and that's only the tip of the iceberg. The list goes on, and indeed it's a long one.

But now get ready to sample some of the best examples of early classic vintage blues. Some songs will be familiar, others perhaps not. But they're all terrific and loads of fun to play on the ukulele just as they initially were for me on the banjo and the uke-tuned banjo mandolin. So, full speed ahead and be prepared for the happy side of the blues and the hours of rich enjoyment and entertainment that these songs will generate for you in this book's great collection.

The Delmore Brothers

Introduction

"Woke up this morning, blues all around my bed. Good morning, blues, how do ya do? ..."

The Blues. As All-American as Yankee Doodle and Mom's apple pie. Simplicity itself in their basic form. Just 12 bars. Repetitious and predictable. And yet the blues have generated one of the largest outputs of music heard around the world. From their beginnings in the plantations of the deep rural south to the concert halls of Carnegie and the Royal Albert in London, the blues have held sway for well over 100 years and are still going strong.

What makes these songs that adhere to such a restricted structure yet remain so different, so distinct and enduring? What wellspring of emotion do they tap? What universal response is embedded in their simple words and basic musical form?

Like the sentiments of the 1926 song The Birth of the Blues maybe the inspiration comes from the "breeze in the trees" or the notes of a "whippoorwill out on a hill." More likely it's the strain of a broken heart, the two-timing ways of an unfaithful lover, betrayal and rejection, the oppression of poverty, or any one of a thousand human hardships and miseries.

The feeling is expressed so well in a recent magazine photo of an elderly black man holding his guitar and quoted as saying:

"If it ain't been in a pawn shop it can't play the blues."

Rising up from the lonesome picking and singing of a solitary acoustic guitar player or the plaintive sound of a blues harp bending its notes like the wail of a distant train whistle, the blues have come a long way. Predominantly from African-American sources and performers – from slaves, sharecroppers, field hands, riverboat roustabouts –the songs have evolved from chants, shouts, work songs, spirituals, folk songs, and a multitude of other varied sources. They worked their way up from New Orleans to the Mississippi Delta, to Memphis, to Kansas City, Chicago and the world beyond. From the primitive sound of homemade instruments, the blues have steadily moved on through the resonance of early jazz, rhythm & blues, rock and roll, to the screaming output of amplified electric guitars.

Let's take a closer look at this unique phenomenon called the blues. We've already seen that its fundamental form consists of 12 measures. Now we'll see that these are arranged in a fixed progression of chords, although there can be slight variations. Here's the basic 12-bar "true" blues, key of C, 4/4 time:

C	C	C	C7
F	F	C	C
G7	G7	C	C

A common variation of blues chords can be seen in the following chart.

C	F or G7	C	C7
F	F	C	C
G7	F	C	C

A popular "New Orleans" variation follows this chord progression:

C	F or G7	C	C7
F	F#dim7 or Fm	C	A7
D7	G7	C	C

In some blues songs every chord is played as a seventh. Various "cadences" (endings) can be found in the final two measures.

The comment was once raised to a prominent cornet jazz player that a number of blues all sounded the same. He took immediate exception and pointed out that such thinking came from a chordal standpoint and not a melodic one. Although the chord structure of basic blues may remain set with little variation, what emerges when the melody kicks in is distinctive and individual. And, of course, not all blues adhere to the 12-bar format.

Although minor chords often appear in blues songs that don't adhere to the strict 12-bar structure, seldom if ever do minor chords substitute for the majors in basic 12-bar blues. This seems odd since one might think that minor chords would better convey a melancholic mood and sense of sadness.

A popular vocal form of traditional blues is a three-line stanza, the first two lines repeated, then a different third line. Repetition of the second line emphasizes the emotion:

> *I hate to see that evening sun go down, (2X)*
> *'Cause my lovin' baby done left this town.*

> *Feelin' tomorrow like I feel today, (2X)*
> *I'll pack my trunk, make my getaway.*

> *My man's got a heart like a rock*
> *cast in the sea, (2X)*
> *Or else he wouldn't have gone so far fro me.*

> *Corinna, Corinna,*
> *where you been so long? (2X)*
> *Ain't had no lovin' since you been gone.*

Just because a song has the word Blues in the title doesn't mean the 12-bar format will be followed. Anything goes, the variety is endless. But the underlying concept remains the same: they all reveal some emotion of sadness, anguish, or worry. Occasionally, however, a blues like The Boll Weevil can put a humorous spin on a tongue-in-cheek situation.

Interesting twists and turns can exist within a blues song. Royal Garden Blues, for example, contains two blues, one basic blues in the key of C, then a New Orleans style in the key of G. The original recording of the Tin Roof Blues by the New Orleans Rhythm Kings also includes within the same song two blues formats in the same key, one traditional and the other New Orleans style. Beale Street Blues has two parts, the first doesn't fit the 12-bar form, but the second part does, a true traditional blues.

In the days following the Jazz Age – in the years before, during and after World War II – the blues entered the field of popular music, notably in 1941 with Harold Arlen and Johnny Mercer's Blues In The Night, now considered a pop standard. The song hit the charts, stayed there for 11 weeks, and reached the #1 spot. It was recorded by all the well-known vocalists of the day – Cab Calloway, Dinah Shore, Julie London, Ella Fitzgerald, Rosemary Clooney, and there were others, and still are.

Big Bands "swung the blues" – Count Basie, Glenn Miller, Benny Goodman, Duke Ellington, all the greats. Then there was that form of the blues called Boogie Woogie – "eight to the bar" - and the country was jumpin' and jivin' like it never had before. The Andrew Sisters hopped on the bandwagon and sang it with The Bugle Boy from Company C. Arthur Smith's 1945 recording of Guitar Boogie sold three million copies and took the country by storm. The blues were definitely on a roll.

With the 1950s came rock and roll, and the influence of the blues cannot be overstated. From the earliest days of rock right up to the present, the blues have provided a venue for some of the world's most legendary performers including B.B. King, Elvis Presley, Ray Charles, Eric Clapton, Stevie Ray Vaughn, Joe Bonamessa, Jimi Hendrix, Taj Mahal, and Johnny Cash with his Folsom Prison Blues.

These giants of contemporary music – and there are so many more – carry on the tradition of blues artists some of whose roots go back a hundred years, like Bessie Smith and Ma Rainey. In the 1920s and 30s the torch was carried by Blind Lemon Jefferson, Son House, Leadbelly, and Robert Johnson who allegedly sold his soul to the devil in exchange for guitar virtuosity. More recently came the contributions of the Beatles, Janis Joplin, Bob Dylan, and jazz players like Louis Armstrong and Wynton Marsalis.

From all indications the blues are here to stay, and we wouldn't want it to be any other way. Surely new song themes will arrive, new performers will emerge, new blues bands will be heard, but that formidable influence of 12-bars will live on, perpetuating itself as it has for generations. The beat goes on – and hopefully ever more shall do so.

New Orleans Rhythm Kings

B.B. King

ALCOHOLIC BLUES

EDWARD LASKA   Ukulele tuning: gCEA   ALBERT VON TILZER

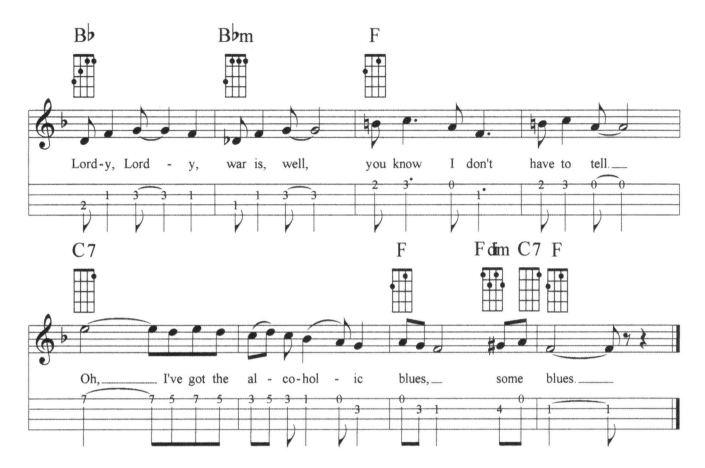

In 1919, the same year as Alcoholic Blues was written, Congress passed the 18th Amendment to the Constitution which probibited the manufacture, distribution and sale of intoxicating beverages. Owing to Andrew Volstead, Chairman of the House Judiciary Committee, who introduced the legislation, it was informally known as the Volstead Act, more commonly as Prohibition. After 14 years, the law was repealed in 1933 by the 21st Amendment.

AUNT HAGAR'S BLUES

J. TIM BRYMN

Ukulele tuning: gCEA

W. C. HANDY

Old Dea-con Spliv-ins, his flock was giv-in' the way of liv-in' right.
"Why all this raz-zing, a-bout the jazz-ing? My boys have just come home

Said he, "No wing-ing, no rag-time sing-ing here to - night."
with lat-est mu-sic, they play it on the sax-o - phone."

Up jumped Aunt Ha-gar, and shout-ed out with all her might!
"Oh my, just lis-ten!" the dea-con shout-ed with a moan.

AUNT HAGAR'S BLUES

BEALE STREET BLUES

Ukulele tuning: gCEA

W.C. HANDY

BEALE STREET BLUES

BLUES MY NAUGHTY SWEETIE GIVES TO ME

Ukulele tuning: gCEA

Words & Music by:

ARTHUR N. SWANSTONE, CHARLES R. McCARRON, CAREY MORGAN

BLUES MY NAUGHTY SWEETIE GIVES TO ME

BLUIN' THE BLUES

Ukulele tuning: gCEA

SIDNEY D. MITCHELL

H.W. RAGAS
of the Original Dixieland Jazz Band

Down in Sa - van - na lives a fel - low known as Ho - san - na Clay.
And when Ho - san - na plays a dance for you, you can - not re - fuse,

___ How that fel - low could play. ___ He has those pi - an - o keys a - moan - in'
___ you just wear out your shoes. ___ He play pi - an - o so sweet you dance till

blue har - mo - nies ___ all day. ___ He drives your sor - rows a - way.
your wear - y feet ___ re - fuse ___ to lift up both of your shoes.

BLUIN' THE BLUES

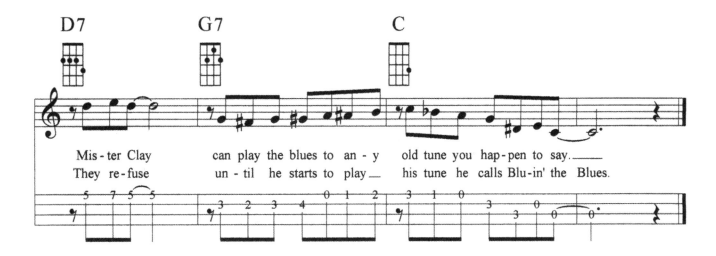

Mis - ter Clay / can play the blues to an - y / old tune you hap - pen to say.____
They re - fuse / un - til he starts to play___ / his tune he calls Blu-in' the Blues.

THE BOLL WEEVIL

Ukulele tuning: gCEA

TRADITIONAL

2. The next time I seen the boll weevil
   He was sitting on the square,
   The next time I seen the boll weevil
   He had all his family there,
   Just a-lookin' for a home,
   Just a-lookin' for a home.

THE BOLL WEEVIL

3. The farmer took the boll weevil
   Put him in the red hot sand,
   Boll weevil said to the farmer,
   "I can take it like a man,"
   This'll be my home,
   This'll be my home."

4. The farmer took the boll weevil
   Put him on a block of ice,
   Boll weevil says to the farmer,
   "This is mighty cool and nice,
   This'll be my home,
   This'll be my home."

5. The farmer took the boll weevil
   Put him in the fire,
   Boll weevil says to the farmer,
   "This is just what I desire,
   This'll be my home,
   This'll be my home."

6. Boll weevil said to the farmer,
   "You had better leave me alone,
   I ate up all your cotton
   Now I'll eat up all your corn,
   I'll have a home,
   I'll have a home."

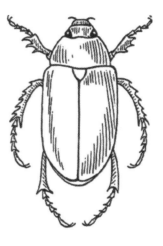

7. The merchant got half the cotton,
   The boll weevil got the rest,
   Didn't leave the farmer's wife
   But one old cotton dress,
   And it's full of holes,
   And it's full of holes.

8. Farmer said to his wife,
   "Now what d'ya think of that?
   The boll weevil made a nest
   In my old Stetson hat,
   Now it's full of holes,
   Now it's full of holes."

8. If anyone should ask you
   Who it was who sang this song,
   Say an Oklahoma farmer
   With a pair of blue jeans on."
   Now he's lookin' for a home,
   Now he's lookin' for a home.

BOOGIE WOOGIE

Ukulele tuning: gCEA

TRADITIONAL

"Boogie Woogie" is a style of music made popular in the 1920s mainly for the piano. In reality it is nothing more than an up-tempo form of the classic 12-bar blues.

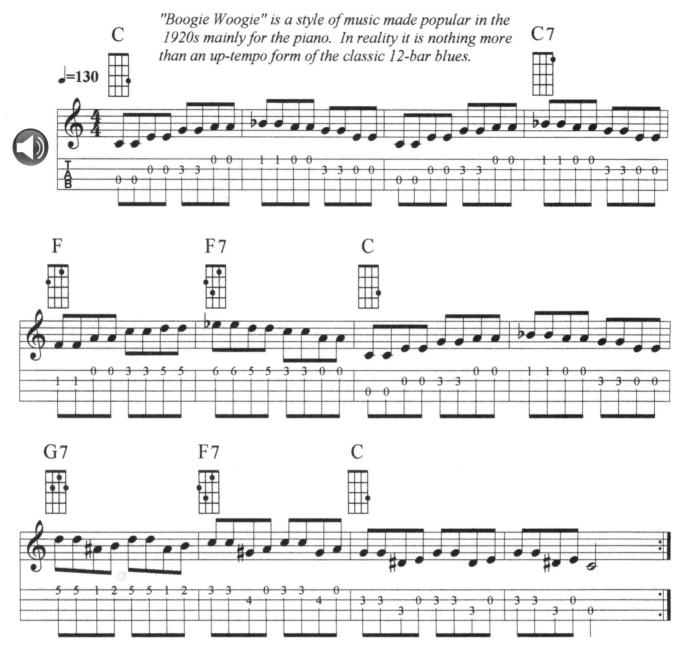

Characteristic of the Boogie Woogie is a repeated figure that continues through the chord changes. On the piano, this pattern is written in the bass clef and played with the left hand, the right hand playing an overlapping melody or blocking chords. Observe the number of notes in each measure — "eight to the bar." A typical left hand figure can be found in the last four measures of this sample Boogie.

C. C. RIDER

Ma Rainey recorded this song in 1924 under the title of "See See Rider." Another popular title variation is "Easy Rider." It's a classic 12-bar blues presented here with a Latin beat.

Ukulele tuning: gCEA

TRADITIONAL

2. Goin' away, baby, won't be back till fall,
   Goin' away, baby, won't be back till fall.
   Find me a good man, won't be back at all.

3. Buy me a pistol, just as long as I am tall,
   Gonna shoot my man and catch the Cannonball,
   If he won't love me, he won't have no gal at all.

DALLAS BLUES

Ukulele tuning: gCEA

HART A. WAND

DALLAS BLUES

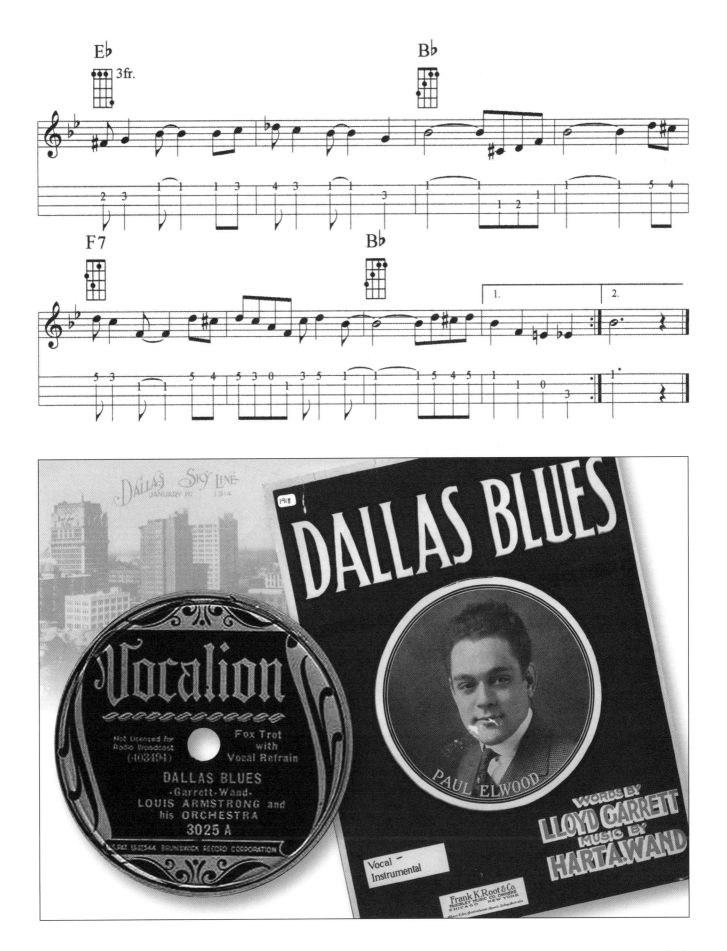

DEEP ELEM BLUES

Ukulele tuning: gCEA

TRADITIONAL

FAREWELL BLUES

Ukulele tuning: gCEA

PAUL MARES
LEON ROPPOLO
ELMER SCHOEBEL

JAZZ ME BLUES

Ukulele tuning: gCEA

TOM DELANEY

JAZZ ME BLUES

JAZZ ME BLUES

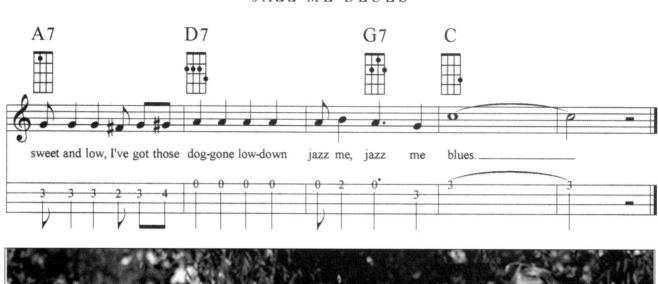

sweet and low, I've got those dog-gone low-down jazz me, jazz me blues.

JELLY ROLL BLUES

Ukulele tuning: gCEA

FERDINAND "JELLY ROLL" MORTON

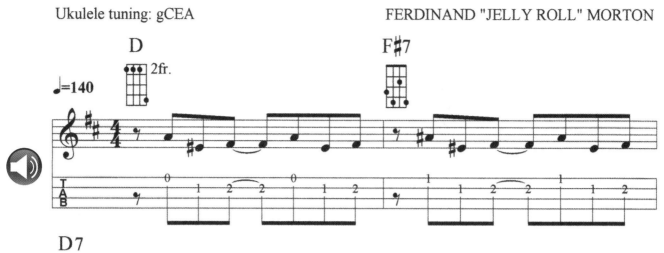

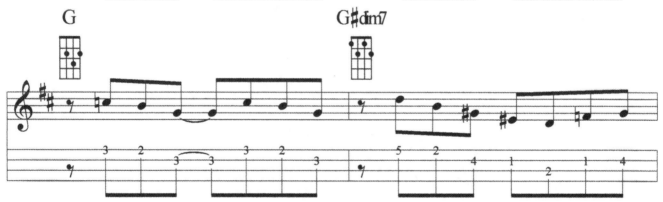

JELLY ROLL BLUES

JOE TURNER
The Folk Song

Ukulele tuning: gCEA

TRADITIONAL

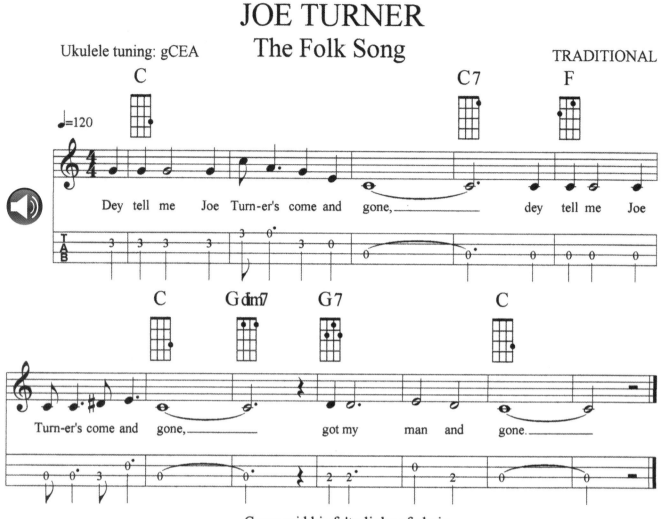

Come wid his fo'ty links of chain,
Come wid his fo'ty links of chain,
Got my man and gone.

Come like he never come befo',
Come like he never come befo',
Got my man and gone.

Allegedly, Joe Turner (aka Turney) was the brother of Pete Turney who was the governor of Tennessee in the 1890s. Periodically, Joe would come to Memphis, round up the local convicts, and escort them to the penitentiary in Nashville. Prisoners were handcuffed to a chain, and appropriately Joe was known as a "long chain man." He was dreaded and despised not only by the convicts but by wives and girlfriends whose husbands and boyfriends Joe would take away.

It is said that this song is the forerunner of all the blues songs that have followed. Its long holds, repetitious notes, and repeated lyrics are characteristic of early Southern "folk blues" that have set the stage for the blues format we know today.

For a powerful recording of the song, check out the YouTube version with Wynton Marsalis and Eric Clapton.

JOE TURNER BLUES

Ukulele tuning: gCEA

W.C. HANDY

LONESOME MAMA BLUES

Ukulele tuning: gCEA

ANNA WELKER BROWN & E. NICKEL

BILLIE BROWN

I've got those lone-some ma-ma blues, since my love has been re-fused,

my poor heart is griev-in' be-cause he is leav-in' me,_____ but wait and see.____

Some day he'll come back a - gain___ on that ver - y same old train. I

know_____ he'll nev-er find_____ an-oth-er gal_____ so good and kind.____

LONESOME MAMA BLUES

MEMPHIS BLUES

Ukulele tuning: gCEA

W.C. HANDY

MEMPHIS BLUES

RED WAGON BLUES

Ukulele tuning: gCEA

DAVE DORSEY

JOHNNY ALLEGRO

I've got those old Red Wag - on Blues, I threw a -

way my worn out shoes, I'm

goin' to hitch my po - nies, for they're my good old cro - nies, they'll

stick thru thick and thin right to the end.

RED WAGON BLUES

ROYAL GARDEN BLUES

Ukulele tuning: gCEA

Clarence Williams & Spencer Williams

ROYAL GARDEN BLUES

ST. JAMES INFIRMARY BLUES

Ukulele tuning: gCEA

TRADITIONAL

ST. JAMES INFIRMARY BLUES

I went down to old Joe's barroom
On the corner by the square,
The drinks were served as usual,
And the usual crowd was there.

On my left stood Joe McGinty,
His eyes were bloodshot red,
He turned to the crowd around him,
And these were the words that he said:

"I went down to St. Jame's Infirmary
To see my Baby there,
She was stretched out on a long white table,
So sweet, so cold, so fair."

Let her go, let her go, God bless her,
Wherever she may be,
You can search this wide world over,
And never find another girl as sweet as she.

There are six men going to the graveyard,
Six in an old-time hack,
Six men going to the graveyard,
But only five are coming back.

When I die, please be sure to bury me
In my high-top Stetson hat,
Put a twenty-dollar gold piece on my watch chain,
So the gang'll know I died standing pat.

I want six crap shooters for my pall bearers,
A chorus girl to sing me a song,
Put a jazz band on my hearse wagon
To raise some hell as we roll along.

And now that you've heard my story,
Let's all have another shot of booze,
And if anyone should happen to ask you,
Well, I've got those gambler's blues.

ST. LOUIS BLUES

Ukulele tuning: gCEA

W. C. HANDY

ST. LOUIS BLUES

This section of the song is unique. Rather that going to the relative minor (Dm) it goes instead to Fm, called the "tonic" minor.

2nd Strain (Minor)

wo-man___ with her dia-mond rings,_____ pulls that

man a - round on her a-pron strings._____ 'Tweren't for

pow-der___ and for store - bought hair,_____ the

man I love___ would not gone no - where._____ Got de

ST. LOUIS BLUES

ST. LOUIS BLUES

1st Strain:

Been to the Gypsy to get my fortune told,
To the Gypsy, done got my fortune told.
'Cause I'm most wild 'bout my Jelly Roll.
Gypsy done told me, "Don't you wear no black."
Yes, she done told me, "Don't you wear no black.
Go to St. Louis, you can win him back."

2nd Strain: (Minor):

Help me to Cairo, make St. Louis myself,
Git to Cairo, find my old friend Jeff.
Gwine to pin myself close to his side,
If I flag his train, I sure can ride.

3rd Strain:

I loves that man like a school boy loves his pie,
Like a Kentucky Col'nel loves his mint and rye.
I'll love my baby till the day I die.

Alternate 3rd Strain:

A black headed gal make a freight train jump the track,
Said a black headed woman make a freight train jump the track.
But a red headed woman makes a preacher Ball the Jack.

Alternate 3rd Strain:

Lawd, a blonde headed woman makes a good man leave the town,
I said blonde headed woman makes a good man leave the town.
But a red headed woman makes a boy slap his papa down.

Alternate 3rd Strain:

Oh, ashes to ashes and dust to dust,
I said ashes to ashes and dust to dust.
If my blues don't get you my jazzing must.

Jelly Roll Morton

STAGOLEE BLUES

Ukulele tuning: gCEA

TRADITIONAL

STINGAREE BLUES
(A Down Home Blues)

Ukulele tuning: gCEA

CLINTON A. KEMP

STINGAREE BLUES

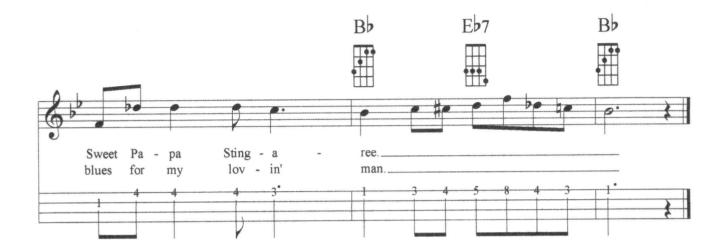

Sweet Pa - pa Sting - a - ree.
blues for my lov - in' man.

Cliff Edwards - known as
Ukulele Ike - was the voice of
Jiminy Cricket in the 1940
Walt Disney film "Pinocchio."

TISHOMINGO BLUES

Ukulele tuning: gCEA

SPENCER WILLIAMS

TISHOMINGO BLUES

WABASH BLUES

DAVE RINGLE

Ukulele tuning: gCEA

FRED MEINKEN

WABASH BLUES

WANG-WANG BLUES

Ukulele tuning: gCEA

Words by:
LEO WOOD

Music by:
GUS MUELLER, "BUSTER" JOHSON, HENRY BUSSE

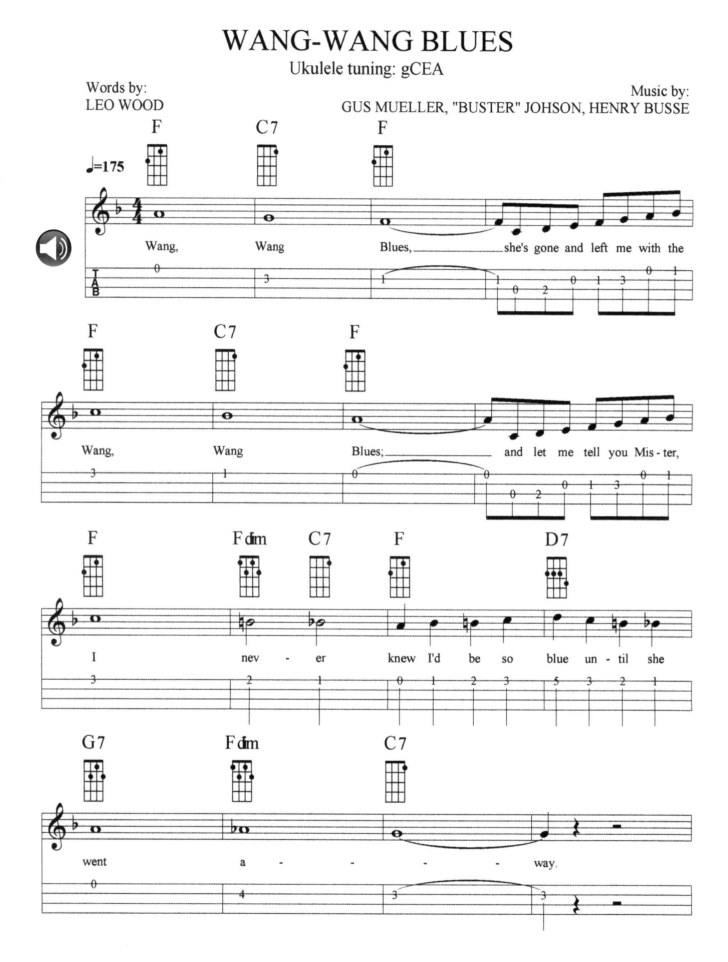

WANG-WANG BLUES

WEARY BLUES

Ukulele tuning: gCEA

ARTIE MATTHEWS

WEARY BLUES

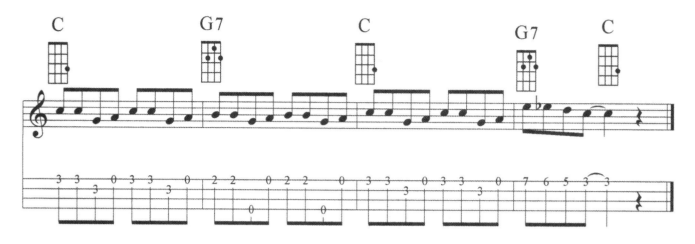

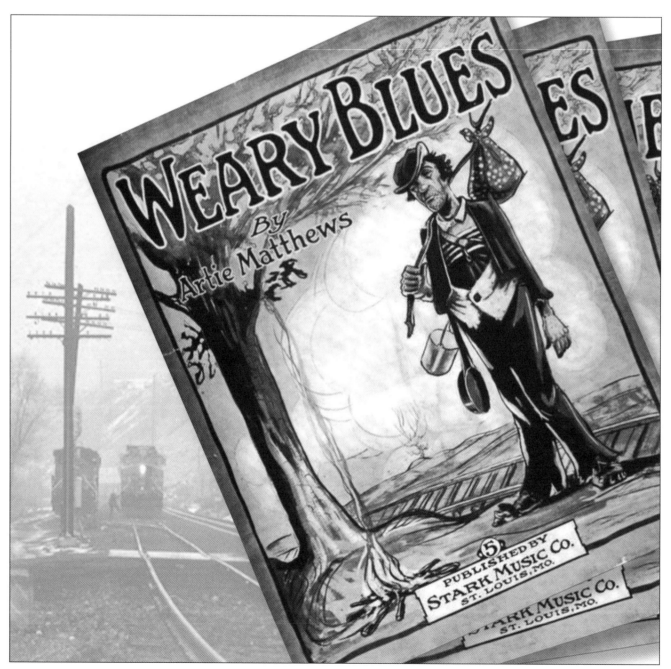

WORRIED MAN BLUES

Ukulele tuning: gCEA

TRADITIONAL

WORRIED MAN BLUES

LYRICS
(As sung by the Carter Family, Woodie Guthrie, Ralph Stanley, and others)

It takes a worried man to sing a worried song,
It takes a worried man to sing a worried song,
It takes a worried man to sing a worried song,
I'm worried now, but I won't be worried long.

I went out to the river, and I lay down to sleep, (3X)
When I awoke there were shackles on my feet.

Twenty-nine links of chain tied arond my leg, (3X)
And on each link the initials of my name.

I asked the Judge, tell me what my fine might be, (3X)
Twenty-one years on the Rocky Mountain Line.

When the train arrived it was 16 coaches long, (3X)
The girl I love is on that train and gone.

If anyone should ask you who composed this song, (3X)
Tell 'em it was I, and I sing it all day long.

Under the title of "A Worried Man" the folk group Kingston Trio recorded this song in 1959 adding new lyrics and giving the song a bouncy upbeat style that is typical of most performances.

The Kingston Trio

YELLOW DOG BLUES

Ukulele tuning: gCEA

W.C. HANDY

YELLOW DOG BLUES

Originally written as the "Yellow Dog Rag," Handy claimed he changed the name after hearing a blues musician at the Tutwiler, Mississippi train station singing the words, "Goin' where the Southern cross the Dog." The reference is to the intersection at Moorehead, Mississippi of the Southern Railroad and the Yazoo Delta Railroad, nicknamed the Yellow Dog.

Although the "Dog" in the title has no animal connotation, many jazz bands in the B part of the song fill measures 3 and 4 with barking, wolf howls, yelping growls, woofs – any other canine sounds that come to mind. Unfortunately the lyrics are not suitable and have been omitted.

SHUFFLE BLUES

Ukulele tuning: gCEA

Chord Diagram Solo

One strum per diagram. Back stroke on second eighth note.

SHUFFLE BLUES
Tablature Chord Solo

Ukulele tuning: gCEA

STAGOLEE BLUES

Chord Diagram Solo

One strum per diagran. Back stroke on second eighth note..

Ukulele tuning gCEA

TRADITIONAL

More Great Ukulele Books from Centerstream...

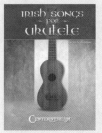

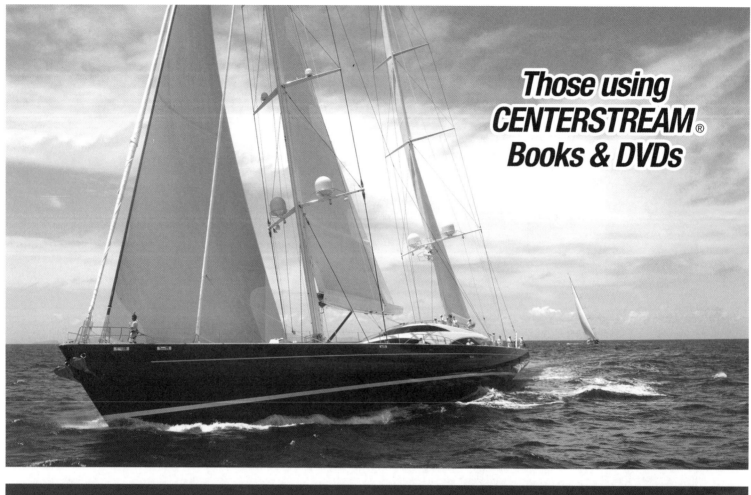